W9-CCO-967

The Beginnings of Science

The Beginnings *of* Science

By Tom McGowen

TWENTY-FIRST CENTURY BOOKS
BROOKFIELD, CONNECTICUT

Cover photograph courtesy of Photo Researchers (© Mary Evans Picture Library)

Photographs courtesy of Visuals Unlimited: pp. 8 (© SIU), 23 (© John D. Cunningham), 26 (© AMAX);
Science Source/Photo Researchers: pp. 13 (© George Holton), 17 (© Lawrence Migdale), 21 (© John Sanford
and David Parker/Science Photo Library), 34 (© John Ross), 37, 67 (Science Photo Library), 71 (© Sheila
Terry/SPL); The Pierpont Morgan Library/Art Resource, NY: p. 19; Scala/Art Resource, NY: pp. 25, 57, 69;
Erich Lessing/Art Resource, NY: pp. 39, 47, 61; LEE60013 Codex Atlanticus f.386r Archimedes Screws and
Water Wheels, 1503/4-7 (pen and ink) by Leonardo da Vinci (1452–1519) Biblioteca Ambrosiana,
Milan/Bridgeman Art Library, London/New York: p. 43; STC90197 Planetary orbits, plate 18 from "The Celes-
tial Atlas, or the Harmony of the Universe" (Harmonia Macrocosmica) depicting the Ptolemeic and Tycho
Brahe systems, pub. by Joannes Janssonius, Amsterdam, 1660–1 (engraving) by Andreas Cellarius (17th centu-
ry) (after) Stapleton Collection/Bridgeman Art Library, London/New York: p. 65

Library of Congress Cataloging-in-Publication Data
McGowen, Tom.
The beginnings of science / Tom McGowen.
p.   cm.
Includes bibliographical references and index.
Summary: Discusses the roots of science as developed by
primitive people, Greek thinkers, Muslim scholars, and those
responsible for the birth of the scientific method in Europe.
ISBN 0–7613–3016–X (lib. bdg. : alk. paper)
1. Science—History—Juvenile literature.
[1. Science—History.]
I. Title.
Q126.4.M34 1998
509—dc21   97–51923
                                             CIP
                                             AC

Published by Twenty-First Century Books
A Division of The Millbrook Press, Inc.
2 Old New Milford Road
Brookfield, Connecticut 06804

Contents

ONE   **What Is Science?**   7

TWO   **Long Ago Beginnings**   11

THREE   **The Wisdom-Lovers of Ancient Greece**   29

FOUR   **A Dark Age and a New Beginning**   49

FIVE   **Modern Science Is Born in Europe**   55

SIX   **From the New Philosophy to Modern Science**   73

For Further Reading   75

Index   77

CHAPTER ONE

What Is Science?

Most people really don't know what science is. They think it has something to do with working with big, shiny machines, and inventing things such as the electric light or laser.

But actually, science is mainly a way of *thinking* about things—of wondering about them, and trying to figure them out instead of just accepting them. Many great scientific discoveries were made because a scientist observed something that most people wouldn't have paid any attention to, and tried to understand it. For example, seeing an apple fall off a tree made English scientist Isaac Newton think about why the apple went down instead of up. In time, he figured out the whole idea of gravity. So, science is a way of trying to determine such things as why an apple falls down or why a leaf is green or why wind blows or what lightning is. It's really a way of trying to gain knowledge about everything in your environment. In fact, that is what the word "science" means—"knowledge."

Scientists gain knowledge about a particular thing in a series of steps. They start with careful study and observation. Then they fit together all the facts they have learned, and use logical reasoning to determine just what

Curiosity and careful observation are essential ingredients of a scientific approach to any topic.

they have found. They generally do experiments to determine the truth of their findings, and use mathematics to measure and verify the results. Finally, they produce an explanation, known as an hypothesis. Nothing they do is based on guesses or on just *believing* they may be right. That is not the scientific way.

It may seem as if gaining knowledge ought to be easy, but that isn't true. It took thousands and thousands of years for people to gain the knowledge we have today of such things as the distance of stars from earth, the structure of atoms, and how magnetism works. For thousands and thousands of years, people didn't even dream of trying to find out about such things. They simply accepted everything as it was, or perhaps they believed old tales and legends that had been handed down for generations. So, because not much knowledge was being gained, nothing much changed. Life stayed just about the same for people everywhere—and generally, it wasn't very easy and often wasn't pleasant. There was always the threat of starvation, caused by droughts or plant-killing blights. There was constant danger of death for tens of thousands or even millions of people from outbreaks of plague or other serious diseases. Even simple, ordinary illnesses often killed people or left them crippled or sickly.

But then, about 450 years ago, what we call science began in Europe, and things started to change. As time went on, things changed faster and faster, because more and more knowledge was being gained. And that increase of knowledge, the result of the work of scientists, made the world we live in today. Because of science, modern farms are able to produce enormous amounts of food. Diseases that used to kill people by the millions have been brought under control. With such advances as anesthetics used in surgery, refrigeration, air-conditioning, and others, science has made life tremendously more comfortable for all of us.

But, how did science ever get started after all those centuries when nothing much changed? Where did it come from? How did it grow?

That's the story you will find here—the story of how science began.

CHAPTER TWO

Long Ago Beginnings

For people who lived in prehistoric times, the world was full of mysteries and terrors. They did not have the knowledge that we have now, and many things that are of no concern to us were puzzling and frightening to them. If a comet appeared in the sky, they feared it was a warning of some terrible event that was going to happen. If they became ill, they believed they were possessed by evil spirits. When winter arrived, they were usually afraid that summer might not come back again!

But there were always some people who tried to figure out answers to mysteries, or who tried to find ways of easing people's fears. They were generally priests or priestesses, or wise old men and women who were regarded as magicians and witches, or sometimes just ordinary people who were looking for the best way of doing something. People such as these learned to make healing potions from plants; to use the movements of the sun, moon, and stars as a calendar; to make new substances with rock, clay, sand, and fire; and discovered how to use numbers and word symbols for keeping records of things. What these people did was the very beginning of science.

Without writing, there could never have been such a thing as science. There would be no way to keep careful records of experiments and discoveries, no good way to pass knowledge from one generation to the next without losing some of it. Writing made science possible. But for tens of thousands of years, there was no such thing as writing anywhere in the world. It was an idea that slowly grew, with one improvement after another.

The concept of writing began when prehistoric people wanted to leave a message or record of something, and used a picture to do it. Perhaps a tribe had a very successful hunt, which meant plenty of food and new clothing for everyone. On the stone wall of a cave, or perhaps on a large rock, someone would paint or scratch some pictures—men with bows and spears, running after many animals. These pictures recorded the memory of the great hunt for the future.

The idea of using pictures to record a happening or give a message became common among prehistoric people almost everywhere. About 5,000 years ago, in a hot land in the Near East, people got the idea of using pictures to stand for words. This was the first kind of writing. The inventors of this picture writing were short, black-haired, rather pudgy people that we call Sumerians. They wrote by making pictures with a pointed stick on flat lumps of moist clay. The clay was then put in the hot sun to make it dry hard.

It was easy to turn some words into pictures. A picture of an object, such as a bird, a fish, or a tree, usually meant the name of the object. But it took imagination to make pictures that stood for most words. For example, a picture of person's head with a bowl close to his or her lips meant "eat."

The problem with this kind of writing is that *lots* of pictures are needed and, at first, the Sumerians had to use more than 2,000 different pictures! Of course, it took a long time to write anything when you had to make hundreds of pictures, so the Sumerians generally used their writing just to make lists of things, such as "two cows—five sheep," in order to keep records of what people owned.

Prehistoric people created these paintings of hunters on the walls of a cave in Africa.

Eventually, the Sumerians and others who used picture writing, such as the Egyptians, got the idea of turning their word pictures into symbols—shapes that could be made very quickly. A quick squiggle might stand for "man," some crisscrossed lines might stand for "house." This made writing easier, but it still required hundreds of symbols. Then, another Near Eastern people, whom we call Semites, thought of using symbols to stand for the *sounds* in their language, which marked the beginning of the alphabet. They needed only about thirty symbols to write any word in their language.

It was now possible to quickly write down anything from a story to an explanation of how to travel from one place to another. And once written language was perfected, science became possible. Now, great ideas and discoveries could be written down and kept, for people to read and learn from, for hundreds and even thousands of years.

NUMBERS AND SHAPES

Counting is not something that people could always do. Like writing, it had to be invented. The idea of counting probably started among prehistoric people, as a way of remembering things, such as the number of days it might take to get from one place to another. People kept track with their fingers; one finger for each day of travel, or one for each animal in a herd. They counted by touching their fingers, one after another.

Because people have ten fingers, ten became the basis for most kinds of counting. In time, people gave special names to the first ten numbers. This made keeping track of things a lot easier. Instead of thinking that a journey might take "as many days as all the fingers on one hand and all the fingers but one on the other," a person could think "nine days." For numbers larger than ten, people might simply say "ten and three," or "ten and eight." For groups of ten, they would say "two tens" or "four tens," and in time these became single words like "twenty" and "forty."

It was probably when people started doing business, such as trading baskets of grain for jars of wine, that arithmetic was invented. A merchant might use a pebble to represent each basket of grain, and if he traded two, he took away two pebbles. Counting the remaining pebbles told him how many baskets were left.

People quickly realized that a pebble or a stick or a cut on a piece of wood could stand for a larger number, such as five or ten, as well as one. This made it possible to do arithmetic with larger numbers. An ancient trader of the Near East, sitting on sandy ground, would draw a line in the sand with his finger. A pebble on the right side of the line stood for a one, a pebble on the left side was a ten. If he had 34 baskets of grain to trade, he could show the number 34 with three pebbles on the left of the line and

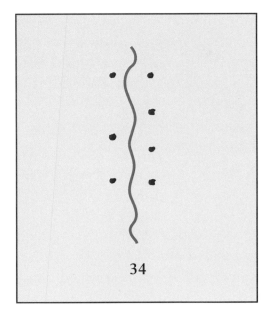

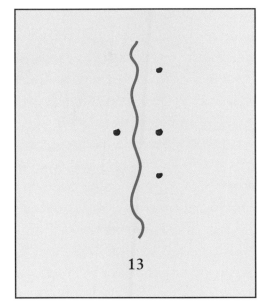

34

13

four on the right. If he traded 21 baskets, he picked up one pebble from the right and two from the left, and he could instantly see that 13 baskets remained.

About the time people started to write by using pictures or symbols for words, they also thought of using symbols for numbers. Usually, a straight line stood for 1, different symbols stood for the other numbers up to 10, there was a special symbol for 10, and special symbols for 20, 30, and so on. People could now write numbers of any size.

When the ancient Egyptians and other people began to build such things as pyramids and palaces, they started paying attention to shapes—squares, rectangles, circles, triangles. A pyramid, for example, was formed by putting the same kind of triangle on each of the four sides of a square. Extending the sides of a square upward to the same height as their length, formed a cube-shaped building.

Builders discovered that some shapes seemed to depend on numbers. Someone, somehow, found that if a length of rope was marked with 12 evenly spaced marks and then tied into a circle, something rather amazing could be done with it. The circle was put on the ground and stakes were pounded in at marks that were three spaces apart. Then, the rest of the rope was pulled out tight and a stake was pounded down at a mark four spaces from one of the other stakes. This formed a perfect right triangle! One side was three spaces long, one was four, one was five.

This was a tremendously useful discovery. For one thing, it formed *corners* for squares and rectangles, and by extending the short sides of a right triangle to whatever length was wanted, the bases of huge pyramids and other buildings could be laid out. In Egypt, people who did this kind of work were known as "rope stretchers."

About 5,000 years ago, in England, prehistoric people began working on the monument of huge standing stones called Stonehenge. The stones that form Stonehenge were arranged in a perfect circle. This could never have been done by chance, so someone must have figured out the mathematical way of making a circle. Probably, a stake was pounded into the ground and a long rope was tied to it. Then, someone stretched the rope out to its full length, and holding onto the end of it simply walked all the way around the stake, keeping the rope stretched tight. Someone else, following the rope stretcher, carefully put down a pebble or made a mark on the ground every few steps. This formed the circle.

So, as long ago as nearly 5,000 years, people had discovered how to make such shapes as circles, triangles, squares, and others. They had learned to add, subtract, multiply, and divide numbers, and had learned how to use numbers to measure things. By the time people could write, and history began, a great deal was known about numbers and shapes, which are the basic parts of what we now call mathematics. And mathematics is one of the most useful tools of science.

SKY WATCHERS

People did not begin building towns and villages until about 10,000 or 12,000 years ago. Before that, for many thousands of years, they generally moved about from place to place, following herds of deer or other animals they hunted for food and gathering up whatever wild plants they could find to eat. They

*Stonehenge is a prehistoric monument formed of giant standing stones
arranged in a definite pattern—a perfect circle.*

were nearly always out in the open, beneath the sky. This made them far more familiar with objects that are in the sky than most of us are today.

The sky was very important to prehistoric people. For many of them, it was the basis of their religion. In some parts of the world, the sun was worshiped as a god, and in other parts it was the moon that was worshiped. These religions, like most, had special holidays and days for feasts and ceremonies. But, how could those people of long ago celebrate a special day each year when they had no calendars? How could they keep track of such special events?

The sun and moon were used to keep track of such things. The sun and moon rise at a different point on the horizon each 24-hour day. If people wanted to have a special religious ceremony or feast on the same day of summer each year, they could watch where the sun rose that day and put up a marker, such as two boulders side by side. Each summer after that, on the day the sun rose exactly between the two boulders, people could have their feast or ceremony knowing that it was the proper day. There are many such boulders, mounds of earth, and other markers, all over the world, put up by prehistoric people to mark a special sunrise or moonrise. Stonehenge, in England, is thought to be just such a sort of "calendar."

Probably as soon as people started to count, they realized that the moon went through a change about every 30 days. It went from being covered by darkness to being a full, glowing circle and then became dark again, taking about 30 days each time. People became aware that in each of these moon-change periods some special thing happened, such as the first blossoming of flowers after the long winter, and this same special thing was repeated every 12 moon periods. In almost every language, each moon period became known by a name describing the special thing that happened during that period. For example, many of the Native American tribes that lived on the plains of North America called the period that we now call the month of April, "Full Sprouting Grass Moon," for this is the month when spring fully arrives, with sprouting grass and flowers.

Thus, the changing moon became a calendar. The number of months that passed from one beginning of spring or one midwinter to the next became a year. People began to plan their lives around the yearly appearance of certain "moons"—the springtime Moon of Planting, when they put seeds into the ground; the autumn Moon of Harvesting, when they gathered

This picture, called "The Manner and Style of Gardening and Planting of the Indians," is from a 16th-century book on natural history. Native American people planned their planting and harvesting by observing the changing moon.

crops and began to prepare for winter; the Full Hunter's Moon, when deer were fattest and most plentiful.

Ancient people also observed the stars. They became aware that stars were grouped together in certain ways, forming distinct shapes. They gave names to these shapes (called constellations), such as "the Great Bear," and "the Swan." They saw that each shape rose above the horizon at a certain time of night, moved slowly across the sky, then sank out of sight, just as the sun and moon did. But these shapes did not stay in the sky all year, like the sun and moon. Different stars and constellations appeared at different times of year, during different seasons. This happens because earth travels around the sun, and the sky and objects we see when it is on one side of the sun are different from what we see when it is on the other side. Thus, new constellations and stars become visible, rising a little higher each night, then sinking down again, as earth moves along its path.

People realized that the appearance and movement of constellations and stars could be used in a number of ways. Many ancient people in different parts of the world used the first rising of a star or the first appearance of a constellation to tell them when to start planting or harvesting. For some, the first appearance of a star or constellation marked a special holiday, or even the start of a new year. It was also discovered that constellations could be used as guides, to help find the way on long journeys over land or sea.

Ancient people who watched the stars and constellations each night quickly noticed some strange objects that resembled stars but didn't act like stars. They did not twinkle as stars do, and unlike stars, they changed in appearance, going from bright to dim and back to bright again. They also seemed to wander across the sky, often passing in *front* of stars. The ancient Greeks called these objects *planetae*, meaning "wanderers," and today we call them planets, taken from that Greek word. The difference between stars and planets is that stars are huge balls of glowing gas, like our sun, while planets are *much* smaller balls of compressed gas or rock. Like earth, the planets are moving in orbits, or paths, around the sun and are fairly close to us, while the stars are incredibly far away.

For prehistoric people, whose religion was based on objects in the sky, studying the sky for any changes or omens was the special duty of certain

This is an artist's impression of the constellation of Scorpio, the Scorpion. The stars that make up the constellation have been enhanced by the artist.

priests. For people who merely used the sky as a calendar to keep track of such things as when to plant, harvest, and hunt, the sky watchers were generally old people who had gained great wisdom during their lifetimes. But whether it was done by priests or elderly "wise ones," this careful observation of the sky was the beginning of the science of astronomy, a word that means "star knowledge."

For days the man's head had been hurting badly, and everything he looked at seemed blurry. He had hoped this would stop, but it didn't, so at last he went to the tribe's healer and told her of his trouble.

"An evil spirit has come to live in your head," she told him soberly. "I think I must open your head and let it out, or else the pain will not stop."

She gave him a potion made of plant leaves that made him feel groggy and dreamy, and made his body feel numb. The healer had him stretch out on the ground, and she called some of the other men to hold him down. Then, with a sharp knife made of stone, she began to cut a hole in his head, at the place where the pain was.

Operations of this sort really did take place many thousands of years ago. The skulls of numerous prehistoric people have been found with small smooth holes in them, made by sharp-pointed instruments of stone. Modern doctors can tell that many of these wounds healed nicely, and the patients survived. We don't know for sure why such operations were done, but chances are good it was to let "evil spirits" out of the head of someone who was having severe headaches. For people of long ago often believed that diseases and illnesses were caused by evil spirits that had gotten into a person's body.

The healers of a tribe or community—men and women who tried to heal the sick and injured—worked out various ways of trying to make the spirits leave a sick person. They might do this by wearing a horrible mask and making loud noises to frighten the spirits away. Or, they might give their patients a potion, a drink made from bitter plant roots, that would make them throw up, carrying the "spirits" out of their bodies.

By making potions out of plant roots, bark, and leaves, healers gradually learned how different kinds of plants and plant mixtures affected people. Some made people sleepy; some made them throw up; some made them numb, so they didn't feel much pain. The knowledge of how to make these potions and what they would do was passed down from one healer to another. To most people, this seemed like magic, but actually, it was the beginning of *medicine*.

Egyptian embalmers removed the internal organs from bodies they mummified. Some mummies were then placed into elaborately decorated cases such as this one.

Prehistoric people regularly cut up animals for food, so healers could easily get a good idea of what was inside an animal's body. The healers of ancient Egypt had particularly good opportunities to learn what was inside a human body. When Egyptian embalmers mummified a body, they took out all the internal organs, and healers could examine them.

However, most ancient healers had no real idea how any of these internal organs worked. They had no idea what the brain did. For the most part, they believed that people's thoughts and feelings came from the *heart*. They didn't know what blood was for, and thought veins and arteries were tubes for letting air move through the body. They didn't know why people's hearts beat, or why they breathed. However, most of them were seriously interested in trying to find out about all these things.

Healers and their patients put a lot of faith in charms and prayers. Prayers were said to the gods, in hope they would take away an illness, and charms were worn to prevent disease or injury from striking. A charm might be an odd-looking rock or bone, or a tuft of bird feathers, kept in a little pouch hanging from a person's neck.

So, healing was connected with magic, religion, and superstition. But healers were beginning to use different kinds of medicines, made from plants, for various sorts of problems. They were also starting to think about how different parts of the body worked. They were building the science of medicine.

BAKING, BURNING, MELTING, AND MIXING

Twenty-five thousand years ago, the people who lived in western Europe depended entirely upon natural substances. Their clothing was made from animal skins, sewn together with needles made of slivers of bone, and thread made of dried tendons from the bodies of animals. Their weapons and tools were made of stone, bone, and wood from trees. They cut and chipped and carved all these substances, but, of course, they could not really change

Early Japanese people discovered that damp clay could be molded and baked into hard containers like this one.

them in any way. Bone was still bone, wood was still wood, skin was still skin.

Then, someone, somewhere, made an interesting discovery. He or she found that certain soft substances, such as the white rock called chalk, the black charcoal of burned wood, the soft reddish rock called iron ore, could be ground into powder and mixed with animal fat. This produced a greasy lump of white, black, or red, that could be rubbed against a flat surface, such as the wall of a cave, and would leave a permanent colored mark. By mixing two natural substances together, a new non-natural substance had been created—paint!

Prehistoric people who lived before about 10,000 years ago probably never dreamed of such a thing as soup. They had nothing to make pots, pans, or kettles *of*, so they really had nothing to make soup *in*. They probably had leather bags or tree bark buckets for carrying water, but they couldn't have put those onto a fire to boil water for soup—the wood or leather would have burned.

But, around 10,000 years ago, people living in what is now Japan made a marvelous discovery. They found that if ordinary soft, damp clay was baked in a fire, it became stiff and hard. They got the idea of shaping moist clay into large round containers and baking them hard. Because these pots could be put onto a fire, meats and vegetables could be boiled in water and soup could be made, as well as other things.

The discovery that copper could be melted, then molded into new forms,
changed the life of people in the Near East in several important ways.

About 6,000 years ago in the Near East, another wonderful discovery was made. Someone found that if a certain kind of shiny red rock (copper) was heated in a fire, it would melt into a thick, shimmering liquid. When this liquid cooled, it became hard as rock again. People quickly realized that they could make the hot liquid cool into almost any shape they wanted, simply by pouring it into a mold. By cutting the shape of a spear point into a block of stone and pouring the liquid into that mold, they could make many good sharp spear points very quickly. This method was much easier than slowly chipping spear points out of pieces of stone, as they had been doing for thousands of years.

Discovering how to melt copper led to the discovery of other kinds of meltable rock, which we now call metals. People soon learned that different kinds of metals could be mixed together when they were hot liquids. When the mixed metals cooled, the mixture was often different from the two original metals. For example, when the two soft metals copper and tin were mixed, the mixture became a much harder metal that made good swords and armor. This was the first *artificial* metal, called bronze.

About 5,000 years ago, people in the Near East found that sand, too, could be changed by fire. Heated in a clay pot over a fire, sand, sometimes mixed with other things, became a syrupy liquid. When the liquid cooled, it was a hard, brittle material that light could pass through—glass! At first, people used glass only for making beads and ornaments, and it was as precious and costly as jewels. In time, glass became easier to produce, and was used for making containers and small bottles.

The discovery of things that could be changed by heating and mixing was tremendously important and useful. Instead of using only stone, wood, and animal bodies to make things from, people could now create artificial substances—paint, ceramics, metal, and glass—that could be used for everything from cooking soup to decorating the walls of a dwelling. The knowledge that substances could be changed by being baked, melted, and mixed together was the start of the science we now call chemistry.

CHAPTER THREE

The Wisdom-Lovers of Ancient Greece

By about 3,000 years ago, people in most of Europe, Asia, and a few other parts of the world had acquired a large storehouse of knowledge from their prehistoric ancestors. They understood arithmetic and had writing. They used objects in the sky for a calendar, and to help them find their way across great distances. They could make pottery, metals, dyes and paints, and glass. They also had begun to learn about how to take care of sickness and injuries.

But, people still thought of the world as a rather fearsome, uncertain place. Because they believed that good or bad "spirits" caused most things to happen, people tried to invent magic to control those spirits. They believed in superstitious explanations for things, not ever wondering if those explanations were really right.

Then, about 2,700 years ago, in one tiny part of the world, something began to happen that hadn't happened anywhere else in all the thousands of years before. In the land of Hellas, which we now call Greece, a few people began trying to make sense of the world without resorting to magic and superstition. Instead of just accepting the world as a mysterious realm ruled by magic, they wanted to find out what *really* made things happen.

These people were known as philosophers, a word made from two Greek words that mean "wisdom-lovers." One of them, a man named Democritus, once said: "I would rather discover one cause of something than be king of Persia!" Another philosopher, named Anaxagoras, when asked what the purpose of life was, answered: "To learn about the sun, moon, and stars!"

The wisdom-lovers were not exactly scientists, but they developed some of the methods of science. They never quite thought of doing experiments, but they carefully watched everything, slowly thought things through, and tried to find sensible, logical explanations. During the hundreds of years when Greece was one of the world's great cultures, these philosophers came up with scores of new ideas. They made discoveries in mathematics, astronomy, and medicine. Centuries later, their ideas helped create science, and many of their discoveries affect our world today.

THE PEOPLE WHO WONDERED HOW EVERYTHING BEGAN

The ancient Greeks were great sailors and explorers. They sailed the seas all around Greece, exploring unknown islands and the shores of foreign lands. Wherever they found a good place for people to live, they started a colony. One of the most important colonies was Ionia, near where the nation of Turkey is located today. The major city of Ionia was Miletus, and it was in Miletus that the Greek idea of science apparently began.

A man by the name of Thales, who lived in Miletus about 2,500 years ago, was probably the first of the Greek philosophers, or wisdom-lovers. He is generally thought of now as the one who started the whole idea of science, by using some of the methods scientists now use.

Thales seems to have been a person who wanted to know the origin of things, how the world had been formed. Most people of his time—Persians, Egyptians, and even Greeks—would have just shrugged and said that everything had been made by the gods. But not Thales. He wanted to know *how* things had been made.

So, he tried to work out answers using common sense. He knew that when a river overflows, it usually leaves new soil on its banks. It seemed logical to Thales that the fresh soil must have been formed *in* the water. Thus, he reasoned that water must be capable of forming things. Thales decided that everything in the world must have been formed out of water. Water, he thought, was the building material of the universe.

There were other wisdom-lovers living in Miletus at the same time as Thales, and some of them were also interested in figuring out how everything had begun. But they came up with different answers than Thales. A man named Anaximenes had noticed that when a person blows warm breath against a cold object, drops of water generally form on the object. Obviously, the water must have come out of the person's misty breath. So, it seemed to Anaximenes that the world, with its water and even its rock and soil, could have been formed out of warm, misty air. For him, warm, misty air was the building material of the universe.

Another philosopher, Anaximander, had yet another idea. Like Thales and Anaximenes, he believed there was one basic material that had formed the universe. But Anaximander thought of the material as a formless, invisible substance that earth, air, fire, and water had come out of. Anaximander believed that the world had once been a watery mass surrounded by intense heat or fire. In time, the heat caused most of the water to evaporate, leaving dry land with bits of water (lakes, seas, rivers) on it. Thus, the world had been formed.

But all the evaporated water must have gone somewhere, Anaximander reasoned. He believed it had formed the clouds and air around the earth. This, he felt, would have caused a great deal of pressure against the layer of fire that had surrounded the watery mass, and the pressure caused the fire to burst. Anaximander believed it was this great explosion of the layer of fire that had formed the sun, moon, stars, and planets. They were actually bits of fire, wrapped in bubbles of air, circling around the world from the force of the explosion.

Anaximander also wondered where people had come from, and he worked out an answer to that. There must have been fish in the watery mass, he thought, and when most of the water evaporated there hadn't been enough left to hold them all. He reasoned that many of the fish must have learned to live on dry land, and in time, they had turned into the different kinds of land animals, including humans. That was where people had come from, according to Anaximander.

Anaximander and the other philosophers had done something that probably no one else had ever done before. Instead of just accepting that everything had been caused by supernatural forces, they had tried to figure out how things could have happened *naturally*. And that is what science is all about.

THE GREEKS WHO LOVED NUMBERS AND SHAPES

About 2,500 years ago, a Greek named Pythagoras started a kind of religious study group. He and his followers, who were known as Pythagoreans, gave up all their money and lived in poverty, eating only vegetables and drinking only water, rather than wine as most Greeks did. They tried to think about only those things that were perfect and holy, and it seemed to them that just about the most perfect and holy of all things were—numbers! The Pythagoreans felt that numbers held the answers to everything. Their motto was: "Numbers are all!"

They did all sorts of things with numbers. At this time, people still used pebbles for counting. The Pythagoreans liked to try counting in different ways, by making numbers into *shapes* with pebbles, like this:

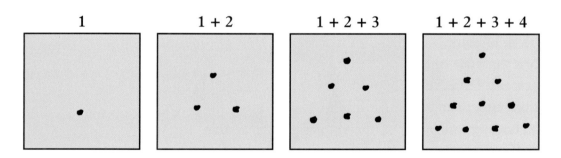

It seemed to them that the last number in that group, 10, was truly perfect, because it contained all the numbers that had gone before it—1 + 2 + 3 + 4 = 10.

They also used pebbles to make "square" numbers, like this:

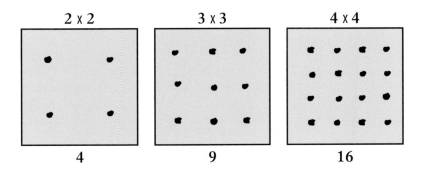

By doing this, the Pythagoreans discovered that a square number is the number you get when you multiply any number by itself. Square numbers led the Pythagoreans to make a surprising discovery. They knew about the Egyptian rope-stretchers' trick of using a circle of rope marked at 12 equal intervals to make a right triangle with one side of three spaces, one of four, and one of five. One of the Pythagoreans, perhaps Pythagoras himself, decided to try working out the square numbers of each side of a right-angle triangle to see if anything new could be learned.

The shortest side of the triangle had three spaces, so the Pythagorean multiplied three by three, getting the square number 9. The next longest

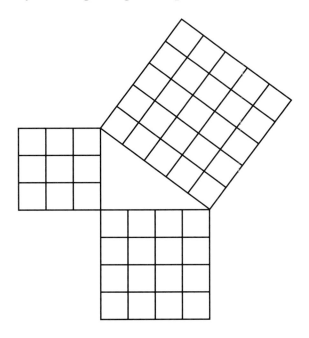

side had four spaces, and four times four produces the square number 16. The longest side, which the Greeks called the hypotenuse, meaning "stretched," had five spaces, and five times five equals the square number 25. What a surprise when the Pythagoreans saw that the squares of the two smallest sides, 9 and 16, added up to 25, exactly the same as the square of the longest side. This became known as the Pythagorean theorem, one of

The famous pyramids of Egypt are solid shapes formed of four similar triangles.

the most famous discoveries ever made in mathematics. (Theorem means an idea that can be shown to be true.)

Just as they experimented with numbers, the Pythagoreans also experimented with shapes. They already knew that different kinds of triangles could be put together to form different kinds of pyramids, and that squares could form a six-sided cube, but they tried other, new things. Working with many kinds of flat shapes made of leather or wood, they also discovered new flat shapes. For example, by putting five equal-sided triangles together so that all the top points touched, they produced a five-sided shape now called a pentagon. They discovered new kinds of solid shapes that could be made from flat ones. One of these was the 12-sided shape called a dodecahedron, each side of which is a pentagon.

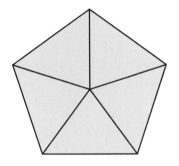 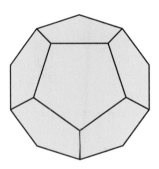

A pentagon (left) is formed from five equal-sided triangles. A dodecahedron is a sphere with 12 flat sides made of pentagons. This diagram shows one-half of a dodecahedron (right), as if you were looking at it from straight above.

The way their experiments with numbers and shapes revealed more and more new secrets and surprises seemed like holy magic to the Pythagoreans. It seemed to them as if *everything* must have some marvelous secret of numbers or shapes hidden in it. In trying to uncover such new secrets, the Pythagoreans came up with some important new ideas.

Most ancient people believed the earth was a flat square or perhaps a dome-shaped mound. The Pythagoreans decided it must be a sphere, or ball. They were absolutely right, of course.

And, most ancient people believed the earth was a special place that was right at the center of everything and never moved. They thought that the sun, stars, and planets all moved around the earth. After all, they could see the sun moving through the sky every day, and see the moon, stars, and planets moving at night. But, not so, said the Pythagoreans. They insisted that the earth was a planet, and moved just like other planets, in a big circle. (The earth and other planets actually move in a kind of football-shaped circle called an ellipse.)

The Pythagoreans came up with these ideas about the earth mainly because of their love for numbers and shapes, and not because they had any proof. They claimed that the earth must be a sphere because a sphere was the most perfect solid shape. And they thought the planets must move in circles because a circle was the most perfect flat shape, the outline of a sphere. Even though the Pythagoreans had no real proof for their beliefs, they had at least come up with some new ideas instead of just "going along" with what most everyone else believed.

Pythagoras is now regarded as one of the world's great mathematicians. Some of the Pythagoreans' ideas and discoveries turned out to be extremely important and useful to scientists who lived centuries later.

TWO GREEKS WHO GAVE US THE IDEAS OF ELEMENTS AND ATOMS

To ancient people, it seemed as if there were really only four kinds of substances—water, air, fire, and earth, which was soil and stone. Some of the first Greek philosophers, like Thales and Anaximander, believed that the world had been formed out of just one of these substances, such as water or air. But a Greek wisdom-lover named Empedocles, who lived almost 2,500 years ago, decided that the world and everything in it was actually made of *combinations* of these four substances.

Empedocles had figured out a way to prove that a substance, such as the wood of a tree, for example, was made out of earth, air, fire, and water. For one thing, wood burned, and Empedocles said that showed there was fire in it. As wood burned it gave off smoke, and Empedocles said that was the misty air coming out of it. The heat of burning wood often caused droplets of water to form on cool objects nearby, and Empedocles insisted that the water had come from the wood. And, when the wood finished burning, all that was left of it was powdery ash, which was a kind of dusty earth, according to Empedocles.

All this certainly seemed to make sense, and a lot of Greek wise men believed that Empedocles was probably right. In time, earth, air, fire, and water became known as "elements"—substances that were pure in themselves, not made of combinations of anything else, but that could combine with one another to form everything else in the universe.

However, some Greek wisdom-lovers did not agree with Empedocles. One of them was Democritus, who lived at about the same time as Empedocles. Democritus believed there were only two things making up the entire universe. One was what he called "the void"—a great endless emptiness, which we now call space. The other was an endless number of very tiny hard objects of many different shapes that formed all the various kinds of things such as water, wood, and rock. Democritus believed that these objects were the very smallest things there were, and could not be cut, broken, or divided in any way to make them smaller. This was why he named them *atoms*, from a Greek word meaning "can't be divided."

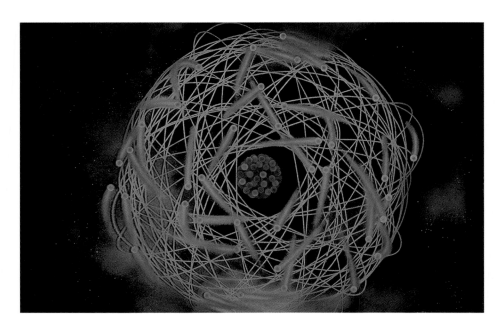

Democritus' belief in atoms guided us to our modern understanding of an atom's structure, as pictured here.

Today, we know that Democritus was right about the void—space—and very close to being right with his idea of atoms. On the other hand, Empedocles was all wrong in his claim that earth, air, fire, and water were elements that formed all other things. Unfortunately, however, Democritus' ideas were more or less forgotten for more than 2,000 years, while Empedocles' idea was believed by most people during that time. Although it was wrong, even Empedocles' idea was useful, for it led to other ideas and important discoveries much later.

THE MAN WHO CHASED AWAY EVIL SPIRITS

In ancient Greece, as well as in much of the ancient world, most people believed that diseases were caused either by evil spirits or by the gods. To cure sickness they tried magical remedies or else prayed to a god to take the illness away.

Some people in ancient Greece became interested in trying to cure diseases in other ways than by prayer or magic. One of the most famous of these was Hippocrates, a doctor who lived about 2,400 years ago. Hippocrates didn't believe evil spirits or gods had anything to do with diseases. He thought that all sicknesses had a natural cause, and they happened because something in a person's body simply went wrong.

Hippocrates started a school for doctors, and he and his students carefully studied many diseases and disorders. They learned to recognize different kinds of diseases by their symptoms, such as chills and fever or pain in a particular part of the body. Hippocrates kept careful records of each kind of disease, its symptoms, and the treatment that worked best on it. No one else had ever done such a thing before.

Hippocrates was a very successful doctor who was able to help, and often cure, many of his patients. Instead of using magic spells or remedies based on superstition to cure illnesses, he urged patients to eat properly, exercise, keep clean, and get plenty of fresh air and sunshine, just as doctors do today! But Hippocrates and his students also knew, from their studies, how to perform many kinds of surgery to help patients, too, if necessary.

*Hippocrates and his students laid the foundations of modern medicine
by observing diseases, recording symptoms, and identifying effective treatments.*

Thus, Hippocrates chased the idea of evil spirits right out of Greek
medicine. By studying diseases and learning natural ways of fighting them,
he truly created the idea of medicine as a *science*.

• THE HIPPOCRATIC OATH •

The ideas of Hippocrates are still important and well known in the world today.

Among the writings of Hippocrates that have survived to modern times are some that deal with the way a doctor should *be*. They say that a doctor should do his or her best to prescribe only treatments that will help a patient. They advise a doctor not to do anything that might cause harm to a patient. And, they urge doctors to live an honorable, dignified life, so that patients will respect them and have confidence in them.

Today, in many medical schools around the world, when young doctors graduate, they repeat words that have come down from the time of Hippocrates, words known as the Hippocratic Oath. An oath is a solemn promise, and the new doctors are promising to follow the advice and suggestions that are given in the writings of Hippocrates.

A TEACHER WHO WAS INTERESTED IN EVERYTHING

On a day some 2,300 years ago, two women walked down a street in the Greek city of Athens, on their way to the market. As they turned a corner they saw a crowd of men moving slowly toward them. One of the men was talking steadily in a loud voice. The others listened to him closely as they walked along. "Look," said one of the women. "Here come the 'walkabouts,' and their teacher, Aristotle."

The "walkabouts" were a group of students who got their name because they often walked about in the part of Athens where their school was located. Their teacher, Aristotle, who ran the school, walked with them, presenting ideas to discuss, answering questions, and explaining things.

Aristotle is regarded as one of the greatest of all the Greek wisdom-lovers, and one of the greatest thinkers who ever lived. He was interested in just about everything—why things always fell *down,* why flame always burned *upward,* what comets were, what made things move. He worked out answers to such questions, producing many new ideas. Aristotle also added his own thoughts to the ideas of other wisdom-lovers.

Some of Aristotle's greatest ideas dealt with what is known as logic. Logic is a way of thinking things out very carefully, using certain rules. With logic, it is possible to tell for sure whether a statement is correct or not. For example, someone might say, "Even though penguins cannot fly, they are birds." How can we tell if that is a correct statement? Using logic, it can be done like this:

A Birds are the only creatures that have feathers.
B Penguins have feathers.
C Therefore, penguins *are* birds.

Aristotle also did a lot of important work in what is now called biology, the science of living things. He studied many different kinds of animals carefully and wrote clear descriptions of the way they lived. He even did tests on various animals, to try to learn how they saw, heard, and felt things.

Most ancient Greeks of Aristotle's time thought that all animals were completely different from one another. Aristotle was one of the first to realize that many kinds of creatures that seemed different were actually related. In fact, he was the first person to work out a way of sorting animals into related groups. Scientists use just such a system today, although Aristotle's crude system has been refined by scientists who came later.

Aristotle wrote a great many books on all the things that interested him, from astronomy to politics. His ideas played a tremendous part in the building of science, and many of them, especially in logic, are still useful today.

Of all the wisdom-lovers, Archimedes was most like what we would now call a scientist. He was the first person we know of who tried to prove his or her ideas by thinking up experiments to test them, as most scientists now do.

Archimedes lived almost 2,300 years ago in the city of Syracuse on the island of Sicily, off the southern coast of Italy. Sicily was a Greek colony then, and like the other wisdom-lovers, Archimedes was a Greek. He loved mathematics and thought of himself mainly as a mathematician. He believed that mathematics could be used to reveal all the mysteries of the universe.

Using mathematics, Archimedes discovered a great deal about machinery, particularly "laws" that showed how levers and pulleys could be used to lift almost anything. In his lifetime, most people regarded him as a famous inventor of machinery, and to this day he is best known for an invention called the Archimedes' screw, a machine for drawing water out of a river, pond, or well to irrigate farmland. This device is still used in many parts of the Near East.

A famous legend about Archimedes reveals how he thought about things in order to solve problems. According to this legend, Archimedes was trying to determine whether silver was mixed within a crown that seemed to be made of pure gold. He realized that the answer lay in finding the *volume* of the crown—the actual amount of metal forming it. Silver is less dense, or lighter, than gold. So, if some silver was mixed with the gold, there would be more metal in the crown, altogether, than there would be in a piece of pure gold that weighed exactly as much as the crown. But the problem was, how to *measure* the volume.

Archimedes decided to take a bath while he thought about this. As he eased himself into the tub, he noticed that some of the water rose up around him and sloshed over the sides. Instantly, he had the answer to the problem! He realized that the weight of his body had pushed up an amount of water that was equal to his body's volume! So all he had to do in order to find the crown's volume was put the crown in a basin of water and measure the amount of water it pushed up. Then, he could put a piece of pure gold that

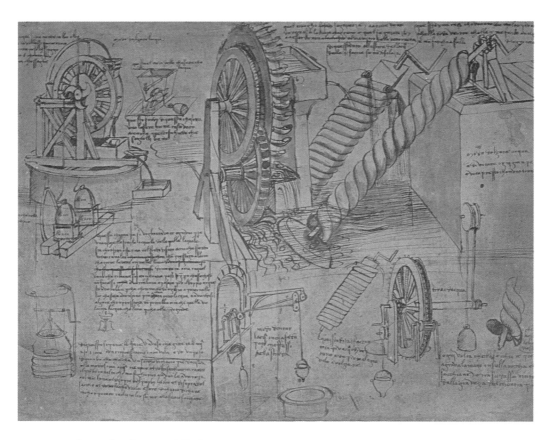

A notebook page filled with pen and ink sketches by Leonardo da Vinci includes 4 different views of Archimedes' screws (right).

weighed as much as the crown into the water, and measure the water *it* pushed up. If there was a difference between them, the crown wasn't made entirely of gold. The legend goes on to tell us that Archimedes was so excited that he jumped out of the bath and ran out into the street—stark naked— triumphantly yelling, "I've got it! I've got it!"

The legend may not be entirely true, but it does show how a great scientist's mind works. Noticing how his body caused water to rise in the tub made Archimedes realize how volume could be measured. Most people would not have paid any attention to a little thing like this. Yet, it led someone with a scientific mind to make a great discovery.

About 2,300 years ago, a Greek army led by the famous conqueror Alexander the Great conquered Egypt. Alexander had a city built and named it Alexandria. In time, Egypt became a Greek possession, ruled by a Greek king, and Alexandria became one of the greatest cities in the ancient world. A center for education and study, with a great university and a library of more than 400,000 books, Alexandria was the home of a number of famous Greek wisdom-lovers. Alexandria was also the place where an important idea was born.

At that time, people in Greece and Egypt believed in Empedocles' old idea that everything in the universe was made out of different combinations of the four elements—earth, air, fire, and water. Some of the wisdom-lovers in Alexandria thought that if they could change just one of the elements that was in a substance, they might be able to create a completely new substance. They knew that substances could be changed by heat. For example, fire could turn wood into ash, and heat could cause metal to melt and turn into a liquid. So, they started trying different ways of heating many different substances, to see what would happen.

They made several observations. They found that when some metals were slowly heated, the metals became covered with a powdery substance. Also, when some kinds of liquids were boiled until all the liquid had evaporated, a powder or muddy material was left behind. And, they discovered that when some solid materials were heated, they turned to vapor. When the vapor cooled, it became a liquid.

Over a period of time, the wisdom-lovers invented special kinds of ovens and pots to enable them to do their work better and more easily. Many of them also wrote books about the things they were doing. In the books, they described their methods and their discoveries.

Most of these wisdom-lovers were Greeks, or half Greek and half Egyptian, but they thought of themselves as Egyptians. For many centuries, Egypt had been known by the name of Chem. As a result, the wisdom-lovers called what they were doing *chemeia,* a word that meant something like "the art of Chem." It is from that ancient word *chemeia,* that we get our word "chemistry." In fact, the Greek-Egyptian wisdom-lovers of Alexandria, heating things in containers and studying the results of what happened, were the first true chemists.

THE EMPEROR'S DOCTOR

By 1,850 years ago, the nation called Rome had conquered Greece, Egypt, and most of the ancient world. As a result, the most important and powerful person in the world was Commodus, the emperor of the Roman Empire. He ruled over millions of people throughout Europe and the Near East. But even an emperor could get sick and need a doctor, and naturally he would have the very best doctor there was. Commodus' doctor was a Greek named Galen, who was said to be the best doctor in the Roman Empire.

In many ways, Galen was much like the Greek wisdom-lovers of earlier times. He not only wanted to cure diseases, he also wanted to know why diseases happened and why things went wrong with people's bodies. At this time, doctors knew very little about how different parts of the body worked. By careful observation, Galen did the best he could to try and find out.

It was against the law to dissect human bodies, even to find out things about them, so Galen studied the bodies of animals, particularly apes. He tried to discover the purpose of each part of an animal's body, hoping that would help him understand human anatomy. He examined hearts, lungs, blood vessels, and other internal organs of animals, and he made some important medical discoveries.

Before Galen, doctors had thought that the little tubes called arteries, running through the bodies of animals and humans, contained only air. But Galen discovered that there was blood in arteries. He also found that blood passes through the heart, although he didn't understand how that happened.

Because Galen did not have a microscope or any of the other useful instruments that doctors now have, he couldn't always see what was really happening. In most cases, Galen just guessed about how the body works. Some of his guesses were very wrong. He wrote books about his discoveries and ideas, and while there were mistakes in them, there was also good new information. Galen's books played a large part in adding knowledge to the study of medicine.

THE MAN WHO MADE THE EARTH THE CENTER OF THE UNIVERSE

One of the last of the people who followed the ways of the Greek philosophers was Claudius Ptolemaeus, who is now known as Ptolemy. A mathematician and philosopher, Ptolemy lived in Alexandria, Egypt, about 1,800 years ago. He wrote a huge book, of 13 parts, that contained all his ideas and discoveries, as well as the thoughts of Greek astronomers who had lived before him.

Ptolemy agreed with most Greek astronomers who thought that the earth was the center of the universe. He pointed out that everything that *fell*, whether rain, waterfalls, landslides, or objects thrown into the air, fell *to* the earth. Ptolemy claimed that things always fall to the lowest place. Because everything falls to the earth, Ptolemy concluded that the earth must be the lowest place, or the center of the universe.

A few Greek wisdom-lovers had thought that the earth moved around the sun, but Ptolemy disagreed. His mathematics showed that if the earth were moving, something thrown straight up in the air ought to come down quite a distance away from the person who had thrown it, because the moving earth would have carried the person away from the point where the object had been thrown. But the fact that an object thrown straight up came straight back down, proved that the earth didn't move a bit, according to Ptolemy.

So, Ptolemy, like most of the ancient Greek philosophers, believed that the earth was the unmoving center of the universe, with everything else moving around it. About 570 years before Ptolemy, a Greek wisdom-lover by the name of Eudoxus had presented the idea that the sun, moon, stars, and planets were all stuck onto a number of huge hollow spheres, or globes,

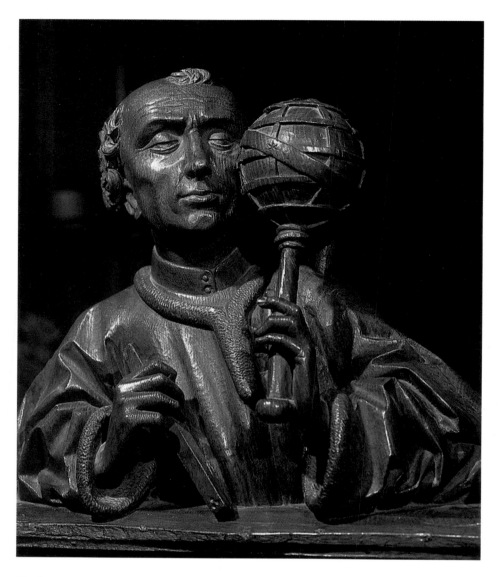

Ptolemy was an astronomer, philosopher, geographer, and mathematician whose calculations seemed to prove that earth was the center of the universe.

that enclosed the earth, one inside another. Using mathematics, Eudoxus showed that these globes revolved, which was why objects in the sky appeared to move around the earth in a circle. Aristotle and other wisdom-lovers had agreed with this idea. Aristotle claimed the spheres must be

IF IT HADN'T BEEN FOR PTOLEMY, COLUMBUS MIGHT NOT HAVE DISCOVERED AMERICA

Ptolemy drew a map of the world for his book about geography. The map did not show North and South America, because no one in Ptolemy's time knew of them. Neither continent had been discovered. But Ptolemy's map showed China sticking out much farther into the Atlantic Ocean than it really does. The map also showed the Atlantic Ocean as much smaller than it really is. This made it look as if it would be very easy to get to China from Europe by sailing across the Atlantic. It was this very map that convinced Christopher Columbus he could do just that. So, if it hadn't been for Ptolemy's incorrect map, Columbus might never have gone on the voyage that led to the discovery of the Americas in 1492.

formed of crystal (natural glass). Ptolemy also used mathematics to determine that there were nine spheres, and to show how the sun, moon, stars, and planets moved on each of them.

Ptolemy also wrote a geography book that contained maps he had made, and described the world as it was known in his time. Centuries later, this book became a major source of information for European scholars and explorers. But it was Ptolemy's writings on astronomy that affected the way people in Europe and the Near East thought about the universe and their place in it for the next 14 centuries. Ptolemy's mathematics seemed to prove that the earth was the center of the universe, with everything going around it in circles. That was what most people believed for the next 1,400 years.

CHAPTER FOUR

A Dark Age and a New Beginning

When Galen and Ptolemy were alive, the Roman Empire was the world's greatest power. It ruled most of southern Europe, part of Britain, the lands along the north coast of Africa, and much of the Near East. People lived peacefully under Roman law, and the powerful Roman army kept things in order.

There were no Romans who were much like the Greek wisdom-lovers, but, nevertheless, education was considered important in the Roman Empire, and Roman scholars studied the ideas and discoveries of the Greeks. The books of Aristotle, Archimedes, and the others were translated into Latin, the language of Rome, and put into colleges and libraries throughout the empire. Thus, the Roman Empire preserved the knowledge of the Greek philosophers.

But a few hundred years after the time of Ptolemy, the Roman Empire began to come apart. There were terrible riots and civil war. Law and order came to an end. The Roman Empire in Europe was invaded by a number of German tribes and was soon broken up into little kingdoms ruled by

German chieftains. In the Near East, parts of the empire were conquered by the Persians.

Without law and order, with fighting going on and people simply trying to survive, such things as schools and libraries were all soon closed and abandoned. Some were destroyed by bands of marauding warriors, or by people who looted them for anything that could be carried off. Most of the books, including those of the Greek wisdom-lovers, were destroyed as well. Only a few remained, stored away in monasteries and churches in Europe and the Near East. In time, the knowledge and ideas of the Greek philosophers were no longer known to most people.

The Roman Empire came to an end in the year A.D. 476, which marked the beginning of what has been called the "Dark Ages." For hundreds of years, most people in Europe and much of the Near East lived in ignorance and superstition, just like the people of prehistoric times. There were no schools, no teachers, no doctors, and the whole idea of science seemed dead.

THE NEW EMPIRE

About 160 years after the fall of the Roman Empire, something of tremendous importance happened in the Near East. A new religion appeared, the religion known as Islam, begun by an Arab named Muhammad. Throughout Arabia, people were converted to Islam by the hundreds of thousands. They were so proud and happy with their new religion that they wanted it to become the religion of the whole world. So, armies of fierce desert warriors came thundering out of Arabia into other parts of the Near East, conquering and making the conquered people join the religion of Islam. They took over Persia (now Iran), Egypt, and other nearby lands, and in the year 711 crossed the Mediterranean Sea and invaded Spain, which they conquered by 718.

The followers of Islam, who were known as Muslims, created a new empire. And like the old Roman Empire, the Muslim empire brought peace, law, and order into the lands it ruled. Life became a great deal safer, easier, and better for most people in the Muslim empire.

This meant that study and education were possible again. Schools and other places of learning were formed. Some of the books of the Greek philosophers that had been preserved during the Dark Ages had been found, and Muslim scholars began to study the ideas and discoveries of Aristotle, Galen, Ptolemy, and the other wisdom-lovers. As a result, throughout much of the Near East and in Spain, the idea of science was reborn.

THE SECRET SOCIETY OF METAL-CHANGERS

Not long after conquering the city of Alexandria, in Egypt, the Muslims discovered old books on *chemeia*, the "Egyptian art," which had been written hundreds of years before, by the Greek-Egyptians. The Muslims put their Arab word *al*, meaning "the," in front of *chemeia*, and turned it into *alchemeia*, a new word in their language. Many Muslim scholars became fascinated students of *alchemeia*.

About A.D. 900, some of these *alchemeia* scholars formed a secret society called the "Brothers of Purity." Apparently, they were a lot like the Greek Pythagoreans had been, some 1,500 years before them. But instead of believing that shapes and numbers were holy, the Brothers felt that the study of *alchemeia* was holy.

The Brothers of Purity believed the old Greek idea of Empedocles and Aristotle that everything was formed out of the four elements: earth, air, fire, and water. They thought that the four elements possessed certain qualities of hotness, coldness, wetness, and dryness, and that it was different mixtures of these qualities that produced every kind of substance there was. For example, sulfur, a dry, yellow, rocklike material that burns easily, was believed to be formed out of the hotness and dryness of the elements fire and earth. Mercury, or quicksilver—the thick silvery liquid found inside some kinds of thermometers today—was believed to be formed out of the coldness and wetness of the elements air and water. The Brothers of Purity believed that all of the earth's metals were formed out of combinations of sulfur and mercury. They thought that the kind of metal that was formed depended on the *purity* of the sulfur and mercury that it contained.

This led the Brothers of Purity to believe that if they could mix the very purest sulfur with the very purest mercury, they could produce what seemed to them to be the most perfect of all metals—gold. They began to look for ways of making absolutely pure sulfur and mercury. The Brothers decided this could only be done with a kind of magical substance they called *al-iksar*, which simply meant "the dry material" in Arabic. In an attempt to find this *al-iksar*, they experimented with scores of different substances; burning, baking, melting, and mixing everything from bones to mustard!

The Brothers never found their magic powder, but they did learn a great deal from their experiments, and they discovered how to make a number of useful things, including varnish and dyes. Several books described the ideas and methods of the Brothers of Purity. These books were of great importance in helping to build the science of chemistry, because they stressed the value of doing experiments in order to gain knowledge.

A NEW WAY OF WRITING NUMBERS

The Muslims did not get all their new knowledge and ideas from the ancient Greeks. Some came from their neighbors in India.

The edge of the Muslim empire lay right at the border of the vast country of India, so there was a lot of contact between the Muslims and the Indians. Naturally, they learned things from each other. And one of the things that Muslim scholars learned from their Indian neighbors was a way of writing numbers that had been invented by the mathematicians of India.

The Muslims used the Arab way of writing numbers that took a lot of symbols. The Indian way was amazingly quick and easy. It required only ten simple symbols, one for each of the numbers from one to nine, and one that stood for zero. With these ten symbols, the Indians could write any number from one to millions. (As you may have guessed, this way of writing numbers forms the basis for the way numbers are written today.)

During the 800s, an Arab mathematician named Muhammad ibn musa al-Khwarizmi studied the Indian number system and wrote a book that explained how to use it. The book also showed how to do a new kind of mathematics that had been developed in India, and that could be used for solving number problems in which one or more numbers was unknown. Al-Khwarizmi called this *al-jabr*, which meant something like, "the science of reuniting," in the Arabic language.

Muhammad al-Khwarizmi's book was tremendously important in helping science get started. It spread the word about the way of writing numbers that is now used throughout the world, and about the form of mathematics that al-Khwarizmi called *al-jabr*, which became one of the most useful tools of science. Today, we call it algebra, and it is used by scientists everywhere.

CHAPTER FIVE

Modern Science Is Born in Europe

The Muslims had conquered Spain in A.D. 718, and by the 900s they had turned it into one of the richest and most civilized countries in Europe. In the capital city of Córdoba there were 70 libraries, a university, and at night the streets were lit by streetlights—which no other city in Europe would have for several hundred years.

At this time, Muslims, Jews, and Christians were living and working together throughout northern Spain. European scholars, many of them monks or priests, were studying the scientific ideas of the Muslim world, most of which had come from ancient Greece. When these scholars returned to their countries in Europe, they brought with them books by Muslim astronomers, mathematicians, doctors, and students of *alchemeia*, as well as copies of the books written by the Greek wisdom-lovers. These were translated into languages that could be read by people of different countries. Thus, ideas and ways of thinking about things that had not been known in Europe for centuries came trickling back in. Some entirely new ideas found their way to Europe, as well.

One of the new ideas that came into Europe was *alchemeia*, which became known as alchemy. Thousands of people became wildly interested in it. For hundreds of years to come, throughout Europe there would be men, and a few women, who spent most of their time laboring over glowing furnaces, stirring bubbling pots, and studying old books. A great deal of astrology, magic, and superstition was involved in the work of these people, who were known as alchemists. For the most part, they were trying to make a magic substance that was called "philosopher's stone," which was like the *al-iksar* that Muslim alchemists had been seeking. No one knew exactly what it was, but it was supposed to be able to turn lead into gold. Many alchemists spent all their money trying to find out how to make it, and wound up poor. A few alchemists claimed to have actually discovered how it was made, and got wealthy by selling the secret to others. Thus, alchemists were generally thought of by most people as either fools or fakers. Many artists and writers who lived at that time drew pictures and wrote stories that poked fun at alchemy.

Certainly, many alchemists were simply foolish people or tricksters trying to swindle someone. But some of them were seriously trying to find things out, and a few did make valuable discoveries. It was a European alchemist who discovered how to make sugar from barley, and another who discovered the chemical element phosphorus. Alchemists also learned how to make hydrochloric acid and sulfuric acid, which are both very useful in industry and technology today. These people helped create the science of chemistry by showing that the tools and methods of alchemy could be used to learn new things and make useful new substances.

During the Dark Ages in Europe, there had not been much interest in astronomy. Just about the only people paying any attention to the stars were astrologers, persons who believed that stars and planets were actually responsible for most events that happened on earth. Astrologers studied the movements of planets and constellations, but they were not interested in studying the stars and planets themselves. However, when copies of the book by the ancient astronomer Ptolemy became available in Europe, there was a new surge of interest in astronomy. Ptolemy's beliefs—that the earth was the center of the universe, surrounded by revolving crystal spheres that

*Despite a widespread perception that alchemists were either
tricksters or fools, some of them did make useful discoveries.*

held the sun, moon, stars, and planets—became well known, and were accepted as the absolute truth.

Knowledge of medicine had not died out completely in Europe during the Dark Ages. It was kept alive mainly in churches and monasteries, and most European doctors and pharmacists (makers of medicines) were priests and monks. But very little had been learned since the end of the Roman Empire, and a lot had been forgotten. Almost nothing was known about how the human body worked. Most treatments for illnesses were medicines made from the leaves and roots of plants. These were generally pastes that were smeared onto a wound or injury, or liquids that were drunk by the patient.

Copies of the book by the ancient Greek doctor, Galen, started coming into Europe at about the same time as Ptolemy's book, and caused exactly the same result. There was a rush of interest in medicine, and there were soon schools where men could learn to be doctors in most of Europe's big cities. What they learned came almost entirely from Galen's books. It was generally believed that everything Galen had said was absolutely correct, and that no one could possibly know more about what went on inside a human body than Galen had known.

By the 1200's, the ideas and discoveries of the Muslims and ancient Greek philosophers had spread throughout Europe. Universities were now being built in major cities by the church, and by kings and other rulers. Students gathered in these places to study and discuss the new knowledge.

THE MONK WHO DEMANDED MATH AND EXPERIMENTS

Roger Bacon, an Englishman, lived from 1220 to 1292, just when the new knowledge and growth of education was spreading. As a young man, he studied at Oxford University, which had just started up, and became tremendously interested in the ideas of the Greek philosophers and in mathematics. In time, he began to produce some fresh new ideas about how scientific problems—then known as philosophical problems—should be studied.

Bacon insisted that mathematics should be applied to scientific problems, especially in the field of astronomy, where accurate measurements could answer many questions. He also believed firmly in the need for doing experiments to help determine causes of things. One of his most famous experiments took place while he was trying to find the cause of rainbows. Using artificial sprays of water he was able to find that seeing a rainbow depended on the position of the sun in relation to the falling drops and to the person observing the rainbow.

For the last 35 years of his life, Bacon was a member of the Franciscan religious order, a monk. He became well known for his knowledge, and was ordered by the pope to produce a book containing all his wisdom and ideas. Bacon's writings were very important in making other European scholars realize the value of using mathematics and experiments to help solve scientific problems.

But despite the work of men such as Bacon, and even though educaiton was now flourishing in Europe, nothing much happened in science over the next two centuries. No one seemed to want to question any of the information that had come into their possession. It was generally felt that the work of the ancient thinkers held all the knowledge there was, and could not be improved upon. Students merely studied their ideas and did not dream of questioning or doubting them. And so, people continued to believe that the earth was the center of the universe, that the sun, moon, and stars were all stuck onto huge revolving globes of crystal, and that everything was formed of the four elements. Most European alchemists continued to try to find a magical substance that would turn lead into gold, and doctors really didn't know any more about how the human body worked than doctors had 1,400 years before.

Then, something happened that caused a revolution!

THE MAN WHO CHANGED THE WORLD

In the year 1543, a book that truly changed the history of the world was published in Poland. The book was titled in Latin, *De Revolutionibus Orbium Coelestium*, which means "the Revolutions of the Heavenly Spheres," or the movement of the planets. The author was a Polish man named Mikolaj Kopernik, who is known as Nicolaus Copernicus in English.

As a young man, Copernicus became a kind of priest, called a canon, of the Roman Catholic Church. He was very interested in astronomy, and was also a good mathematician. For years he studied the movement of the planets through the sky, and used mathematics to try to find out exactly what shape that movement took. After a time, it seemed to him that the great astronomer Ptolemy had made a very bad mistake in his calculations. Ptolemy had said that the earth did not move, but some of the mathematical calculations that Copernicus had worked out for the other planets seemed to show without a doubt that the earth must move, too. When Copernicus wrote his book about the movement of the planets, he stated positively that the earth moved through space, revolving around the sun, just like the other planets. He asserted that the reason the sun and planets appeared to move around the earth was because the earth was rotating (spinning). He also said that the stars were *much* farther away from earth than anyone had ever thought.

These were *astounding* things for anyone living in the 1500s to say! These statements went against what almost everyone believed in—that the earth lay motionless at the center of the universe, with the sun, planets, and stars moving around it. By saying that the earth moved, Copernicus seemed to be saying that the earth wasn't very important at all.

Unfortunately, on the very day that his book was published, Nicolaus Copernicus died, so he never knew what anyone thought of it. Actually, no one really paid much attention to it, at first. A few scholars read it, and most of them disagreed with Copernicus. They believed his claim of a moving earth was ridiculous, and felt it had been very improper of him to dare challenge the statements of the great Ptolemy.

A few religious leaders also read the book, and a number of them were angered by it. They felt that Copernicus was challenging some of the things that were said in the Bible. Because of that, they regarded the book as dangerous and hoped that it would not be read by anyone.

But as time went on, more and more scholars read copies of the book, and more and more of them began to feel that Copernicus was right. His book showed that a belief, such as the belief in Ptolemy's idea

The beginning of the scientific revolution in Europe can be traced to a book written by Nicolaus Copernicus, and published in 1543.

that the earth did not move, wasn't necessarily right just because it had been accepted for a long time. And if one old belief was wrong, maybe others were, too.

Copernicus' book eventually changed the way that European scholars thought about things. It led many of them to begin challenging and questioning numerous old beliefs about astronomy, alchemy, and nature. They began to realize the importance of making careful examinations and doing experiments to gain real facts. Copernicus' book literally changed the course of history in the western world, bringing about the beginning of what we call the scientific revolution. In the rest of the world, everything went on just about as it always had, but in Europe there was now a change taking place. Modern science had been born!

THE DOCTOR WHO STOLE DEAD BODIES!

Oddly enough, a second book was published in 1543 that also helped cause the scientific revolution. This book was by a doctor, and it dealt with the way a human body works.

The author was Andreas Vesalius, a Belgian. Vesalius was the sort of person who believed in trying to find things out for himself rather than just accepting what everyone else believed. He decided that the only way to find out what went on in a human body was to cut dead bodies open and examine them. In those days, criminals who had been hanged were left hanging, as a lesson to other criminals. Vesalius often arranged to have the bodies of hanged criminals cut down and brought to him so he could dissect them. In this way, he was able to carefully examine the inner parts of human bodies, and see for himself how they appeared to work.

In the mid-16th century, most doctors were convinced that the ancient Greek doctor Galen had known everything it was possible to know about a human body, and had revealed this knowledge in his books. But Vesalius soon discovered that Galen had been wrong about a good many things. In his book, he challenged many of Galen's statements just as Copernicus had challenged Ptolemy. Most other doctors were enraged by this, and Vesalius was bitterly attacked. But his book, like Copernicus', eventually set some doctors to thinking, and they realized that it was wrong to merely accept something because it was *believed*, rather than to find things out for themselves.

BREAKING THE CRYSTAL SPHERES

One of the European scholars who read Nicolaus Copernicus' book was a young Dane named Tycho Brahe, a very wealthy nobleman whose greatest interest was astronomy.

On the night of November 11, 1572, Brahe was out walking when he happened to look up at the sky. He saw something so astonishing that he stopped dead in his tracks. There was a brilliant spot of white light in the sky, shining more brightly than any other star. Brahe was astounded when he realized that this starlike light had not been in the sky the night before. It had apparently just appeared out of nowhere. Brahe thought that it must be a new star that had just been created!

Actually, what he was seeing was the light from a star that had *exploded*. The large spot of bright white light was the flare of the gigantic explosion. But the explosion had not just happened, it had actually occurred about 20,000 years earlier! The star was so far from earth—more than 117 trillion miles—that it had taken 20,000 years for the light of the explosion to reach this world on that night in 1572. Before then, the star was so distant and dim that its light couldn't be seen at all.

However, in 1572, more than 425 years ago, no one knew that stars could explode, so Tycho Brahe believed he was seeing a brand-new star. This seemed absolutely impossible, because at that time, everyone in Europe was positive that nothing in the "heavens," as they called space, could ever change. They reasoned that because God had made the heavens, they must be perfect and unchangeable, so nothing new could ever appear in them. Tycho Brahe was one of the new-style scholars, however, who, like Copernicus and Vesalius, refused to believe old ideas just because most everyone else did. It was clear to him that something new *had* appeared in the heavens—this new star.

Brahe used scientific methods—careful observation, measurements, and record-keeping—to try to find if the new object that had appeared was indeed a star. If it was a star, far out in space, it would not move in relation to other stars, as planets and other objects close to earth did. Using instruments especially built for his purpose, Brahe checked the bright object every night for three straight months and determined positively that it didn't move. It had to be a star.

Of course, other astronomers in Europe had also seen the new bright object. But unlike Tycho Brahe, most of them refused to consider that it might be a star. They could not believe that anything new could appear in the unchanging heavens, and made up fantastic explanations to account for the starlike object. Some suggested that it was merely an odd "gathering" of light in earth's air, and it wasn't actually far out in the heavens at all. Some said it was a sign from God, showing that he was angry!

Tycho Brahe was outraged by such foolishness. He called the astronomers who said such things "thick wits" and "blind watchers of the skies." It enraged him that instead of accepting that something new and exciting had happened, they chose to just keep believing "old" ideas.

Five years later, in 1577, Tycho Brahe made another discovery that challenged the old ideas most astronomers clung to. A comet appeared in the sky, and Brahe measured its movement very carefully, night after night. Because of the belief that nothing in the heavens could change, most astronomers agreed that comets were not *in* the heavens but were actually close to earth, between earth and the moon. Brahe's careful measurements revealed that this comet was much farther away than that—it was farther from Earth than the planet Venus! This was additional proof that new things could appear in the heavens. Even more shocking to astronomers was the fact that Brahe's measurements showed that the comet had to be moving *through* some of the crystal spheres that were supposed to be in the heavens. Such movement would be impossible, of course—unless the crystal spheres were not really there!

Most astronomers simply couldn't accept that possibility. They insisted that Tycho Brahe's measurements were wrong, and the comet was really much closer to earth than he said.

Telescopes had not yet been invented in 1577, and only five planets were visible to astronomers looking at the sky with the naked eye. Tycho

Brahe began to very carefully measure the movements of all five of those visible planets. He was the first astronomer ever to check the movement of each planet every single night, so he compiled the best measurements that had ever been made. After a time, he realized that for the planets to move as they were doing, they simply *couldn't* be stuck onto crystal spheres as Ptolemy had said, because the spheres would bump into each other! Thus, Tycho Brahe had now proved that the crystal spheres could not exist. He had destroyed an idea that astronomers had clung to for 1,400 years, since Ptolemy's time.

This illustration from a book called "The Celestial Atlas" shows planetary orbits as they were explained by Ptolemy and by Tycho Brahe.

Tycho Brahe was one of the first real scientists in the world. The methods he used to measure the movement of objects in space were extremely careful and accurate, and this is exactly the sort of work a true scientist must do. No other astronomers of his time ever bothered to do such precise work; they simply accepted the 1,400-year-old ideas in Ptolemy's book without ever trying to check them. But with his painstaking measurements, Tycho Brahe was able to prove that new objects *could* appear in space, and to show that the crystal spheres everyone had believed in did not really exist. These were major discoveries that helped put the science of astronomy on the right path. In time, all astronomers accepted them.

THE DOCTOR WHO WAS INTERESTED IN MAGNETS

In the early 1600s, the personal doctor of Queen Elizabeth I of England was named William Gilbert. He, too, had read Copernicus' book, and like Copernicus, Vesalius, and Tycho Brahe, he felt that people should learn things for themselves rather than just accepting what was said in the ancient books.

Gilbert was curious about why compass needles always pointed straight north. From about 1582 to 1600, he experimented with magnetism—the force exerted by the magnetic field of a magnet—and in 1600 he published a book presenting all his ideas and discoveries. One of his most astonishing ideas, for most people, was that the earth was a giant magnet, with north and south magnetic poles. He was quite right, and today this is a well-known scientific fact. But he also believed it was the earth's magnetism that made everything fall to earth and that held everything on earth in place, and he was wrong about that. It's gravity, not magnetism, that makes these things happen. Gilbert also discovered that a number of substances, such as sulfur, beeswax, glass, and diamond, could act somewhat like magnets when they were rubbed. Electricity was unknown in 1600, so Gilbert had no way of knowing that rubbing those substances gave them an electrical charge. Even so, his ideas and discoveries were actually the beginning of the scientific study of magnetism and electricity.

Tycho Brahe had a number of assistants to help with all his astronomical work. In 1600 he hired another one, a young German schoolteacher named Johannes Kepler, who was very good at mathematics.

Brahe soon regarded Kepler as one of his smartest helpers. In 1601 he gave Kepler a problem to work on—measuring the orbit (path around the sun) of the planet Mars. This problem had been puzzling astronomers for several thousand years. Many had tried, including Tycho Brahe himself, but no one had ever been able to make a measurement that seemed right.

After working for years to calculate the orbit of the planet Mars around the sun, Tycho Brahe (right) assigned the task to one of his assistants, Johannes Kepler. Kepler discovered that the orbit was an ellipse.

Kepler went to work, very slowly and carefully. When he was finished, he had a measurement that seemed to fit Mars' movement better than any measurement anyone else had ever done. Kepler's measurement was just slightly different from the one Tycho Brahe had made.

Kepler wondered what he had done that had made that little difference. After many years of research, he chanced to remember a mathematical equation he had once worked out, which provided the answer. Tycho Brahe, like all the others, believed Mars' orbit was a circle, and measured it that way. But Kepler now saw that his measurement showed that the orbit was *not* a circle. It was actually an ellipse, a fat oval somewhat like the shape of a football.

Kepler's discovery that the orbit of Mars was an ellipse led him to discover that the orbits of *all* the planets were ellipses. Like the discoveries of Tycho Brahe, this one disproved a belief that astronomers had clung to for thousands of years—that all planets moved in circles. It was another big step toward turning astronomy into a true science.

THE FATHER OF MODERN SCIENCE

The person who literally started the kind of science we have today was born in Italy in 1564. His name was Galileo Galilei, but today he is always called just Galileo.

Modern science is generally known as experimental science because scientists often do experiments to test their ideas. Like most real scientists, Galileo was a person who could think up ways to determine if an idea was right or wrong. He is credited with creating one of the most famous experiments in history to show that an idea most scholars had believed in since the days of Aristotle was wrong. Aristotle had said that a heavy object falls to the ground faster than a light one, and this was what most people of Galileo's time believed. But Galileo insisted that objects fall at the same speed regardless of their weight. To prove this, he is said to have dropped two iron cannonballs of different weights from the top of a tower. People watching at the foot of the tower saw that the balls hit the ground at the same time. Galileo did many other experiments with falling and moving objects.

*In this painting, Galileo demonstrates the use of his telescope
to an audience of prominent men in Venice.*

In 1609, Galileo heard about a new device that had just been invented in Holland—the telescope. People were using telescopes to look at distant objects on land or at sea, but Galileo realized that a telescope could be used to look at things in *space*. He made a telescope for himself, which was simply a matter of putting a magnifying lens at each end of a metal tube. Looking at the night sky with this device, he made some of his greatest discoveries.

Galileo was the first person in history to see that the blurry marks on the face of the moon were actually mountains, valleys, and cratered plains. He realized the moon was a *world*, like earth. When he looked at planets through his telescope, they were larger than if viewed with the naked eye, and he could see that they appeared to be rounded objects, like the moon. Seen through the telescope, stars clearly appeared to be much farther away than the planets, and Galileo realized that Copernicus had been right about that.

On the night of January 7, 1610, Galileo was looking at the planet Jupiter when he became aware of three tiny but bright stars clustered near it. The next night, he was astounded to see that these little stars had changed their positions—they had moved, which stars do not do. After several more nights, Galileo spotted a fourth star. He knew that what he had taken for stars were actually moons circling Jupiter. At once, Galileo saw that Copernicus had been right about everything. Earth *did* move. It and the other planets went around the sun in orbits, exactly as these moons were orbiting Jupiter!

Galileo was a teacher at a university, and he began teaching his students that Copernicus' ideas were right. This got him into serious trouble with leaders of the Roman Catholic Church, who felt that Copernicus' ideas conflicted with the Bible. Galileo was forced to publicly announce that Copernicus had been wrong after all. But it didn't matter. Copernicus' ideas were now spreading, and the scientific revolution was gathering strength.

Galileo's contribution to the science of astronomy was tremendous, and many of the other things he did, such as his experiments with falling objects, virtually started the entire field of science now known as physics. Because of his refusal to simply accept old ideas, his frequent use of experiments and mathematics, and his careful observations of things, he is known today as "the father of modern science."

A Doctor's Amazing Discovery

William Harvey was an English doctor who lived at the time the scientific revolution was taking place. He used the methods of science—observation, experiments, and mathematics—to make one of the most important discoveries in the history of medicine.

Rather than simply accepting the old ideas in the books of Galen, as most other doctors still did, Harvey followed in the footsteps of Vesalius and tried to find things out for himself. He cut open the bodies of small animals such as frogs, to attempt to see how their hearts and other internal organs seemed to work. By 1616, Harvey had become the first person in the world to realize that a heart is a *pump*, and that what it pumps is blood.

William Harvey's study of how blood moves through the human body provided scientists and doctors with actual facts about what we would come to call the circulatory system.

However, he did not understand where the blood was being pumped *to* or where it was coming from when it entered the heart. He found the answer to this puzzle in a scientist's way, by using mathematics—actually, just simple arithmetic. He estimated the amount of blood that a heart pumped out each time it beat, and then multiplied that amount by the number of times a heart beat during a half an hour. From this, he quickly saw that more blood passed through the heart in that time than a body could possibly even hold. He realized that there must be only a certain amount of blood in a body, which the heart steadily pumps through the body, over and over, in a circle.

This discovery of what is now known as the circulatory system could actually have been made any time during the thousands of years before, for Harvey didn't have any better instruments or equipment than Galen had. However, it could only have been made using the methods of science. It was as important a discovery as Copernicus' discovery that the earth moved around the sun had been. It swept away thousands of years of belief in mere guesswork, and provided actual fact. It gave medical science new knowledge that made it possible to save many millions of lives from then on.

CHAPTER SIX

From the New Philosophy to Modern Science

Copernicus, Tycho Brahe, Galileo, and the others started modern science—science as it is known today. They actually turned the world in a different direction by changing the way people thought about such things as the earth's place in the universe. By the middle of the 1600s, the idea of science was firmly established. It was not yet called science however, but was usually referred to as "the new philosophy," because it had expanded out of the "old" philosophy of the ancient Greeks. Those who followed the ideas of the new philosophy—refusal to simply accept old beliefs, careful study and checking of facts, creating experiments to find out the truth of things, and using mathematics to prove those truths—were the first true scientists, and helped make our world the way it is today. Their work in the early 1600s led to what is known as the Age of Reason, or the Enlightenment, in the late 1600s and the 1700s, when Isaac Newton of England developed a law of gravitation and a model of the universe, and Antoine Lavoisier of France finally solved the mystery of burning. And these discoveries in their turn led to an ever-expanding increase of knowledge that has continued to this day.

So, the science of today is fairly new, really only some 450 years old. Nevertheless, it owes a debt to prehistoric times, to people who learned to make things out of clay, sand, and metal, who watched the sky, who tried to heal others, who invented counting and writing. It owes a large debt to the Greek philosophers of 2,500 years ago, who loved gaining knowledge more than anything else, and to the Muslim scholars who recovered the wisdom of ancient Greece. It owes a debt to the scholars of medieval Europe, such as Roger Bacon, and to the medieval alchemists in their smoky, smelly cellars. The thoughts, dreams, and efforts of all those people were the beginnings of what we now call science.

For Further Reading

Beshore, George. *Science in Early Islamic Culture*. Danbury, CT: Franklin Watts, 1998.

Gay, Kathlyn. *Science in Ancient Greece*. Danbury, CT: Franklin Watts, 1998.

Harris, Jacqueline. *Science in Ancient Rome*. Danbury, CT: Franklin Watts, 1998.

Parker, Steve. *Galileo and the Universe*. New York: Chelsea House, 1995.

Woods, Geraldine. *Science in Ancient Egypt*. New York: Franklin Watts, 1988.

Index

Page numbers in *italics* refer
to illustrations.

Age of Reason, 73
alchemy, 51-52, 56, *57*, 62, 74
Alexander the Great, 44
Alexandria, 44, 51
algebra, 53
alphabet, 13
Anaxagoras, 30
Anaximander, 31-32, 36
Anaximenes, 31
Archimedes, 42-43, 49
Archimedes' screw, 42, *43*
Aristotle, 40-41, 47-49, 51, 68
arithmetic, 14, 29
astronomy, 21, 30, 48, 56, 58, 59,
    62-68, 70
atoms, *37*, 37-38

Bacon, Roger, 58-59, 74
biology, 41
Brahe, Tycho, 63-68, *67*, 73
bronze, 27
Brothers of Purity, 51-52

calendar, 18, 29
cave paintings, *13*

Celestial Atlas, The, 65
ceramics, 25, *25*, 27
charms, 24
chemistry, 27, 44-45, 52, 56
circles, 15-16
circulatory system, 71-72
clay, 25
Columbus, Christopher, 48
comets, 64
Commodus, Emperor, 45
constellations, 20, *21*
Copernicus, Nicolaus, 60, *61*, 62,
    63, 66, 70, 72, 73
copper, 26, *26*, 27
counting, 14

Dark Ages, 50, 51, 56
Democritus, 30, 37-38
De Revolutionibus Orbium Coelestium
    (Copernicus), 59-60, 62
diseases, 9, 38, 39, 45
dodecahedron, 35

earth, 35-36, 46, 56, 60, 62, 66
education, 49, 58, 59
Egyptians, 13, 15, 16, 23, 24, 33,
    44-45
electricity, 66

elements, 36-38, 44, 51
Empedocles, 36-38, 44, 51
Enlightenment, 73
Eudoxus, 46, 47
evil spirits, 22, 29, 38, 39
experiments, 8, 59, 62, 68, 70, 71

Galen, 45-46, 49, 51, 58, 62, 71
Galileo Galilei, 68, *69*, 70, 73
geography, 48
Germans, 49-50
Gilbert, William, 66
glass, 27, 29
gravity, 7, 66
Greeks, 20, 24, 29-43, 49-51, 58, 74

Harvey, William, *71*, 71-72
healing, *22-24*
Hippocrates, 38-40, *39*
Hippocratic Oath, 40
holidays, 18, 20
hypotenuse, 34
hypothesis, 8

Imhotep, 24
Indians, 52
Ionia, 30
Islam, 50

Japanese, 25
Jupiter, 70

Kepler, Johannes, *67*, 67-68

al-Khwarizmi, Muhammad ibn musa, 53

Lavoisier, Antoine, 73
Leonardo da Vinci, *43*
logic, 41

machinery, 42
magnetism, 66
"Manner and Style of Gardening and Planting of the Indians, The," *19*
Mars, 67-68
mathematics, 8, 16, 30, 42, 46, 47, 52-53, 58-59, 70, 71
medicine, 22, 24, 30, 38-40, 45-46, 58, 71-72
metals, 26-27, 29, 51-52
Miletus, 30, 31
moon, 18, 31, 46, 48, 58, 70
Muhammad, 50
mummies, *23*
Muslims, 50-53, 55, 58, 74

Native Americans, 18, *19*
Newton, Isaac, 7, 73
numbers, 14-16, 32-35, 52-53

observation, 7, *8*, 71

paint, 25, 27, 29
pentagon, 35
philosopher's stone, 56
physics, 70

picture writing, 12-13
plague, 9
planets, 20, 31, 36, 46, 48, 58, 60, 64-65, 67-68, 70
prayers, 24
prehistoric people, 11-16, *13*, 18-24, 74
Ptolemy (Claudius Ptolemaeus), 46, *47*, 48, 49, 51, 56, 60, 65, 66
pyramids, 15, 16, *34*
Pythagoras, 32, 36
Pythagoreans, 32-36, 51
Pythagorean theorem, 35

rectangles, 15-16
religions, 18, 20
Romans, 45-46, 49-50
rope stretchers, 16, 33

science, defined, 7
Scorpio (constellation), *21*
seasons, 18, 20

Semites, 13
shapes, 15-16, 32-35
space, 37-38
Spain, 55
squares, 15-16, 33-34
stars, 20, 31, 36, 46, 48, 58, 60, 63-64, 70
Stonehenge, 16, *17*, 18
Sumerians, 12, 13
sun, 18, 31, 36, 46, 48, 58, 60, 70
symbols, 12-13, 15

telescope, *69*, 70
Thales, 30-31, 36
triangles, 15-16, 33-35

Venus, 64
Vesalius, Andreas, 62-63, 66, 71

walkabouts, 40-41
writing, 12-14, 29